HOW SITTING IN THE RESTROOM CAN IMPROVE YOUR LIFE

"Rejuvenate and Reset: Harnessing the Restorative Power of Restroom Seclusion for a Better Life"

BLESS P. WALTON

TABLE OF CONTENTS

CHAPTER 1
THE UNEXPLORED SANCTUARY

1.1 Introduction to Restroom Seclusion

In the hustle and bustle of modern life, finding moments of solitude has become a luxury. As we navigate through our busy schedules, the restroom, a seemingly mundane space, emerges as an uncharted territory for tranquility and self-discovery. This chapter delves into the intriguing concept of restroom seclusion, exploring the profound impact it can have on our well-being.

The restroom, traditionally viewed as a utilitarian space for personal hygiene, takes on a new dimension when considered as a sanctuary for solitude. It is a place where the daily chaos outside can be momentarily suspended, allowing individuals to reconnect with themselves. This introduction sets the stage for a journey into the unexplored potential of this often-overlooked space.

1.2 The Overlooked Potential of the Restroom Space

Beyond its utilitarian purpose, the restroom harbors a unique potential for providing a mental and emotional retreat. This section unravels the layers of possibility within these confined walls. The isolation offered by the restroom creates a physical and mental distance from external stressors, fostering an environment conducive to introspection.

The restroom's simplicity becomes its strength, offering a blank canvas for individuals to paint their thoughts and emotions. It is not merely a place for bodily functions but a canvas for the mind—a refuge where one can temporarily detach from the demands of the external world. From the soft hum of the exhaust fan to the gentle flow of water, every element within this space contributes to the creation of a serene cocoon.

Furthermore, the restroom is a space of neutrality, free from the clutter of personal and professional obligations. It is a sanctuary that remains constant, providing a sense of stability in a world characterized by unpredictability. This section invites readers to reconsider the restroom as more than just a functional necessity and instead embrace its potential as a haven for mental rejuvenation.

1.3 Breaking Stereotypes: Going Beyond the Obvious

Stereotypes often confine our perceptions, preventing us from recognizing the hidden gems in the ordinary. In this section, we challenge the conventional notions surrounding the restroom and encourage readers to break free from these preconceived ideas. The restroom is not merely a pitstop for bodily functions; it is a space where one can pause, reflect, and reset.

Breaking free from stereotypes involves reimagining the restroom as a versatile environment that goes beyond its conventional role. It is a private retreat that accommodates various activities, from reading a captivating book to practicing mindfulness meditation. By breaking away from the stereotype of the restroom as a purely functional space, individuals can unlock its full potential as a place of self-discovery and renewal.

This section also addresses the societal stigma associated with spending time in the restroom for purposes other than its primary function. It encourages readers to embrace the idea that self-care and mental well-being are essential, and the restroom can play a pivotal role in nurturing these aspects of life. By challenging stereotypes, we open the door to a richer, more fulfilling experience within the confines of this seemingly ordinary space.

In conclusion, this chapter lays the foundation for a paradigm shift in how we perceive and utilize the restroom. It introduces the concept of restroom seclusion as a gateway to mental and emotional rejuvenation, challenges stereotypes associated with this space, and sets the stage for a deeper exploration into the transformative power it holds. The restroom, once seen as a mundane necessity, emerges as a sanctuary with the potential to enhance the quality of our lives in ways we may have never imagined.

CHAPTER 2

THE SCIENCE BEHIND SERENITY

2.1 Understanding the Psychological Impact

The allure of the restroom sanctuary is not merely anecdotal; it finds solid ground in psychological principles that underscore the importance of solitude for mental well-being. As we explore the psychological impact, it becomes evident that the restroom, often considered a mundane space, has the potential to be a catalyst for profound inner transformation.

Solitude, in controlled doses, has been linked to improved mood, increased creativity, and heightened self-awareness. The restroom, by design, offers a brief respite from the constant barrage of external stimuli, providing a unique environment for solitude. Psychologically, this solitude acts as a reset button for the mind, allowing it to disengage from the demands of the external world and focus inward.

Moreover, the psychological impact of the restroom extends beyond momentary relief. Regular moments of seclusion in this space can contribute to a more sustained sense of calm and clarity. Understanding the psychological underpinnings of the restroom sanctuary is crucial for individuals seeking a practical and evidence-based approach to enhancing their mental well-being.

2.2 Stress Reduction: Exploring the Mind-Body Connection

Stress has become an omnipresent companion in our fast-paced lives, and its detrimental effects on both mental and physical health are well-documented. In this section, we delve into the mind-body connection and how the restroom, through its unique attributes, can serve as a refuge for stress reduction.

The mind-body connection is a complex interplay between our thoughts, emotions, and physical well-being. Chronic stress disrupts this delicate balance, leading to a cascade of negative effects on our health. The restroom, with its quiet and isolated ambiance, becomes a therapeutic space where individuals can break the cycle of stress.

Through practices like deep breathing, meditation, or simply taking a few moments of quiet reflection, individuals can activate the relaxation response, counteracting the physiological changes induced by stress. The restroom's seclusion provides a conducive environment for these practices, making it an accessible and practical solution for stress reduction.

Exploring the mind-body connection in the context of restroom seclusion also highlights the role of sensory experiences. The sound of running water, the soft hum of ventilation, and the visual simplicity of the restroom contribute to a multisensory environment that aids in relaxation.

By understanding and leveraging these sensory elements, individuals can enhance their stress reduction efforts within the comforting confines of the restroom.

2.3 The Neurological Benefits of Moments Alone

The neurological landscape of solitude is a fascinating terrain that intertwines with the restroom's potential as a sanctuary for moments alone. Neuroscientific research suggests that taking time for oneself can lead to significant changes in the brain, influencing cognitive function, emotional regulation, and overall mental well-being.

In this section, we explore how moments of seclusion in the restroom can trigger neurological processes that contribute to a sense of serenity. The brain's default mode network (DMN), associated with self-reflection and internal thoughts, becomes more active during periods of solitude. This heightened activity in the DMN fosters self-awareness and a deeper understanding of one's thoughts and emotions.

Furthermore, restroom seclusion can facilitate neural pruning, a process through which the brain eliminates unnecessary synaptic connections. This pruning is essential for cognitive efficiency and adaptability. The restroom, by providing a quiet space for introspection, becomes a facilitator of this neural refinement, contributing to improved cognitive function and emotional resilience.

Neurotransmitters such as dopamine and serotonin, often associated with positive emotions, also come into play during moments of solitude.

The restroom's role as a sanctuary allows for the release of these neurotransmitters, promoting feelings of pleasure and contentment. Understanding the neurological benefits of restroom seclusion adds a scientific layer to the experiential aspects, reinforcing its potential to positively impact mental well-being.

In conclusion, the science behind serenity in the restroom is a compelling narrative that intertwines psychological principles, the mind-body connection, and neurological processes.

By understanding the profound impact that moments of seclusion can have on the brain and overall mental health, individuals can approach the restroom not only as a functional space but as a scientifically validated sanctuary for rejuvenation and reset.

CHAPTER 3
CRAFTING YOUR PERSONAL OASIS

3.1 Redefining Restroom Decor

The ambiance of a space plays a pivotal role in shaping our experiences within it, and the restroom is no exception. This section invites readers to reconsider restroom decor, moving beyond its functional aspects and embracing a design philosophy that fosters tranquility.

Redefining restroom decor involves a departure from the clinical and sterile aesthetics commonly associated with this space. Instead, individuals are encouraged to infuse elements that resonate with their personal sense of calm. Soft lighting, soothing color schemes, and tactile textures can transform the restroom into a welcoming haven. Consider the impact of nature-inspired decor. Incorporating plants or nature-themed artwork can evoke a sense of connection with the outdoors, bringing a touch of serenity to an otherwise utilitarian space. The restroom, often neglected in terms of design, becomes an extension of one's personal style and a reflection of their commitment to well-being.

Beyond visual aesthetics, olfactory elements also play a crucial role in crafting a serene atmosphere. Aromatherapy, through the use of scented candles, essential oils, or diffusers, can introduce a layer of sensory richness to the restroom. Pleasant fragrances have the power to evoke positive emotions and enhance the overall experience of seclusion.

3.2 Practical Tips for Creating a Tranquil Space

Transforming the restroom into a tranquil space goes beyond decor; it involves thoughtful considerations of practical elements that contribute to a serene environment. This section provides practical tips for individuals looking to optimize their restroom for moments of seclusion.

- Clutter-Free Zones: A cluttered space can be mentally overwhelming. By keeping the restroom tidy and organized, individuals create a visually calming environment that promotes relaxation.

- Comfortable Seating: If space allows, consider introducing comfortable seating to the restroom. A cozy chair or cushioned stool can transform the space into a comfortable retreat for extended moments of solitude.

- Soft Lighting: Harsh, bright lighting can be jarring. Pick delicate, warm lighting to make a relieving air. Dimmable lights or the addition of candles can further enhance the ambiance.

- Personal Touches: Infuse the space with personal touches that bring joy. This could include artwork, photographs, or items that hold sentimental value. These elements serve as reminders of positive experiences and contribute to a sense of well-being.

- Soundscapes: Use sound to your advantage. Consider incorporating calming sounds, such as gentle music or nature sounds, to create a peaceful auditory backdrop. This can drown out external noise and further isolate the restroom as a sanctuary.

- Use of Textures: Introduce soft textures through towels, rugs, or even a plush robe. The tactile experience can enhance the overall comfort and contribute to a sense of luxury.

These practical tips empower individuals to customize their restroom space, tailoring it to their preferences and needs. By thoughtfully curating the environment, the restroom becomes a personalized oasis, ready to offer moments of respite from the demands of daily life.

3.3 Transformative Rituals: Making the Most of Your Time

Once the physical environment is optimized, the focus shifts to the transformative rituals that can elevate restroom seclusion to a holistic well-being practice. This section explores a range of rituals that individuals can incorporate into their restroom routine for a more meaningful and rejuvenating experience.

- Mindful Breathing: Utilize the restroom as a dedicated space for mindful breathing exercises. Deep, intentional breaths can have an immediate calming effect on the nervous system, helping individuals release tension and promote relaxation.

- Reflection and Journaling: Keep a journal in the restroom for moments of reflection. Whether jotting down thoughts, expressing gratitude, or setting intentions, this practice encourages self-awareness and mindfulness.

- Reading Nook: Create a small reading nook with inspirational books or calming literature. The restroom can become a retreat for a few pages of a favorite book, providing an escape into a world of imagination and wisdom.

- Digital Detox: Use restroom seclusion as an opportunity for a brief digital detox. Leave electronic devices outside and embrace the solitude without the distractions of screens.

This practice enhances the restorative nature of the experience.

- Grooming as Self-Care: Transform routine grooming activities into self-care rituals. Whether it's a facial mask, a few moments of skincare, or a luxurious bath, these practices turn the restroom into a space for intentional self-pampering.

- Affirmations and Visualization: Use restroom moments for positive affirmations and visualization exercises. Affirmations can boost confidence, while visualization allows individuals to mentally transport themselves to a place of peace and serenity.

By integrating these transformative rituals into the restroom routine, individuals can maximize the impact of their seclusion time. These practices extend beyond the physical space, creating a holistic approach to well-being that encompasses the mind, body, and spirit.

In conclusion, crafting a personal oasis in the restroom involves a multifaceted approach that encompasses decor, practical considerations, and transformative rituals. By redefining the restroom as a space for intentional design and purposeful practices, individuals can unlock its full potential as a sanctuary for rejuvenation and self-discovery. This chapter serves as a guide for transforming the restroom into a haven that nurtures the soul and contributes to a more fulfilling life.

CHAPTER 4

REJUVENATION RITUALS

4.1 Mindfulness Meditation in the Restroom

In the quest for a more serene and balanced life, the restroom becomes a unique canvas for the practice of mindfulness meditation. This section delves into the art of mindfulness, exploring how the restroom's seclusion can be harnessed to cultivate a focused and present state of mind.

Mindfulness meditation, rooted in ancient contemplative traditions, involves bringing one's attention to the present moment without judgment. The restroom, with its inherent privacy and calmness, provides an ideal setting for individuals to embark on this introspective journey. The simplicity of the space, free from external distractions, allows for an immersive experience in the practice of mindfulness.

To engage in mindfulness meditation in the restroom, individuals can start with a few basic steps:

- Find a Comfortable Posture: Whether sitting or standing, choose a posture that feels comfortable and allows for alertness.

- Focus on the Breath: Direct attention to the breath, observing its natural rhythm. This simple act of paying attention to the breath anchors the mind in the present moment.

- Acknowledge Thoughts without Judgment: As thoughts arise,

acknowledge them without judgment and gently guide the focus back to the breath. The restroom's seclusion offers a non-judgmental space for this mental exercise.

- Set a Time Limit: Begin with a manageable duration, gradually extending the time as the practice becomes more familiar.

The restroom, transformed into a meditation space, becomes a refuge for individuals seeking to cultivate mindfulness amidst the challenges of daily life. This practice not only contributes to immediate stress reduction but also fosters a long-term sense of mental clarity and resilience.

4.2 Breathing Techniques for Instant Calm

The breath, a constant companion in our daily lives, holds the key to instant calm and relaxation. This section explores various breathing techniques that individuals can incorporate into their restroom rituals to induce a state of tranquility.

- Deep Belly Breathing: Start by inhaling deeply through the nose, allowing the breath to fill the lungs and expand the diaphragm. Breathe out leisurely through the mouth, exhausting the lungs totally. This technique engages the diaphragm, signaling the body's relaxation response.

- 7-8- 4 Breathing: Hold your breath for seven counts, then quietly inhale through your nose for four counts, and then loudly exhale through your mouth for eight counts. This pattern regulates the breath and promotes a sense of calm.

- Alternate Nostril Breathing (Nadi Shodhana): Using the thumb and ring finger, alternate closing one nostril while inhaling and exhaling through the other. This technique balances the flow of energy and calms the nervous system.

- Box Breathing: Inhale, hold the breath, exhale, and then hold the breath again—all for equal counts. This square pattern of breathing induces a sense of balance and steadiness.

The restroom's seclusion provides an intimate space to practice these breathing techniques without external distractions. Whether as a quick remedy for moments of stress or as part of a regular routine, these techniques empower individuals to tap into the calming power of their breath within the sanctuary of the restroom.

4.3 The Power of Reflection: Journaling for Inner Peace

The act of journaling transcends mere documentation; it becomes a powerful tool for inner exploration and self-discovery. This section explores how the restroom can serve as a sanctuary for journaling, providing individuals with a private space to reflect on their thoughts, emotions, and aspirations.

Journaling in the restroom is not constrained by formalities or structured prompts. It is an invitation to express oneself freely, without judgment or expectation. The act of putting pen to paper allows thoughts to flow, creating a tangible record of the inner landscape.

To harness the power of reflection in the restroom:

- Create a Comfortable Writing Space: Dedicate a corner or use a small portable desk to create a comfortable writing nook within the restroom. Make it inviting with soft lighting and perhaps a scented candle.

- Choose a Journaling Time: Whether it's during a morning routine or as a part of an evening wind-down, establish a consistent time for journaling. The restroom's seclusion provides a reliable and uninterrupted space for this practice.

- Write Freely: There are no rules in restroom journaling. Write about the day's experiences, explore emotions, set intentions, or simply let the pen guide the way. The key is to allow for an unfiltered expression of thoughts.

- Incorporate Gratitude: A restroom journal can also serve as a gratitude journal. Take a moment to reflect on things for which you are grateful. This practice can shift focus towards positivity and contentment.

The restroom, transformed into a haven for journaling, becomes a sanctuary where individuals can navigate their inner terrain. The act of reflection, supported by the restroom's seclusion, offers a path to inner peace, emotional release, and the cultivation of a deeper understanding of oneself.

In conclusion, rejuvenation rituals in the restroom extend beyond the physical environment to encompass practices that nourish the mind and spirit. Mindfulness meditation, breathing techniques, and journaling emerge as transformative tools that individuals can incorporate into their restroom routine for enhanced well-being. As the restroom transitions from a functional space to a sanctuary of self-care, these rituals contribute to a more balanced and fulfilling life.

CHAPTER 5

BEYOND THE RESTROOM - INTEGRATING TRANQUILITY INTO DAILY LIFE

5.1 Carrying the Serenity Outside the Restroom

The transformative power of the restroom sanctuary extends beyond its physical boundaries, seeping into the fabric of daily life. This section explores how individuals can carry the serenity cultivated in the restroom into the various aspects of their day, creating a ripple effect of tranquility.

The transition from the restroom to the outside world can be a delicate moment, and carrying the serenity requires conscious effort. One effective approach is to set a positive intention before leaving the restroom. Whether it's a simple affirmation, a deep breath, or a moment of gratitude, these small rituals serve as a bridge, connecting the inner peace of the restroom to the challenges of the external environment.

Moreover, integrating mindfulness into daily activities can further amplify the impact of restroom seclusion. Whether it's mindful walking, eating, or engaging in conversations, the principles of present-moment awareness cultivated in the restroom can be seamlessly applied to various aspects of life. This intentional extension of serenity becomes a practice in weaving moments of calm into the tapestry of the day.

Carrying the serenity outside the restroom is not about escaping the realities of a hectic world but rather about navigating it with a centered and composed mindset. As individuals step into the chaos of daily life, they can draw upon the reservoir of tranquility cultivated in the restroom, turning ordinary moments into opportunities for mindful presence.

5.2 Nurturing Well-being in a Hectic World

In a world that often prioritizes productivity over well-being, nurturing one's mental and emotional health becomes an essential counterbalance. This section explores strategies for cultivating well-being beyond the restroom, offering practical insights for individuals seeking sustained tranquility in the midst of a hectic world.

- Establishing Mindful Routines: Integrate mindfulness into daily routines, such as morning rituals, meals, and bedtime routines. Infuse moments with present-moment awareness, creating pockets of tranquility throughout the day.

- Digital Boundaries: Set boundaries for digital engagement to prevent information overload and constant connectivity. Designate specific times for checking emails and messages, allowing for intentional breaks from the digital frenzy.

- Nature Connection: Foster a connection with nature, even in urban environments. Take short walks, spend time in green spaces, or introduce indoor plants. Nature has a profound impact on mental well-being and can serve as a source of grounding amidst chaos.

- Prioritizing Self-Care: Incorporate regular self-care practices into the routine. Whether it's exercise, meditation, or hobbies, these activities contribute to overall well-being and build resilience in the face of life's challenges.

- Social Connection: Cultivate meaningful connections with others. Engage in conversations that go beyond surface-level interactions, fostering a sense of community and support.

- Gratitude Practice: Establish a daily gratitude practice to shift focus towards positive aspects of life. This simple yet powerful habit can contribute to a more optimistic and content mindset.

The restroom-inspired well-being extends its influence into daily life by providing a foundation for intentional living. By adopting these practices, individuals can navigate the demands of a busy world while nurturing their mental and emotional health, creating a sustainable approach to well-being that goes beyond momentary escapes.

5.3 Embracing a Restroom-Inspired Lifestyle: Small Changes, Big Impact

The shift toward a restroom-inspired lifestyle involves recognizing the value of small, intentional changes that collectively contribute to a more mindful and balanced existence. This section explores how individuals can embrace this lifestyle, weaving restroom-inspired practices into the fabric of their everyday routines.

- Mindful Consumption: Extend the principles of mindful breathing to activities such as eating. Slow down, savor each bite, and appreciate the sensory experience of meals. This practice not only enhances digestion but also cultivates mindfulness in daily nourishment.

- Digital Detox Days: Designate specific days for digital detox, where screen time is minimized, and the focus shifts to in-person interactions, outdoor activities, or hobbies. This intentional break from the digital world provides a reset for the mind.

- Sensory-rich Environments: Infuse living spaces with sensory elements that evoke tranquility. Soft textures, calming colors, and soothing scents can transform the home into a haven of serenity, extending the restroom-inspired ambiance to every corner.

- Regular Retreats: Incorporate regular mini-retreats into the routine. These can be moments of seclusion, whether in the restroom or another designated space, where individuals engage in rejuvenating practices such as meditation, deep breathing, or journaling.

- Purposeful Pause: Introduce purposeful pauses throughout the day. Instead of rushing from one task to another, take a few moments to breathe deeply, reflect, and reset. These small pauses serve as anchors in a fast-paced day.

- Gratitude Integration: Integrate gratitude into daily life by expressing appreciation for small moments, achievements, or the presence of loved ones. This intentional focus on gratitude cultivates a positive mindset and fosters a sense of fulfillment.

Embracing a restroom-inspired lifestyle is not about drastic overhauls but rather about infusing daily routines with mindfulness and intention. Small changes, when consistently applied, can lead to significant shifts in overall well-being. By adopting a restroom-inspired mindset, individuals create a lifestyle that prioritizes tranquility and resilience in the face of life's challenges.

In conclusion, Chapter 5 emphasizes the seamless integration of restroom-inspired practices into daily life. By carrying the serenity outside the restroom, nurturing well-being in a hectic world, and embracing a restroom-inspired lifestyle, individuals can create a sustainable approach to mental and emotional health.

The restroom, once a secluded sanctuary, becomes a catalyst for a holistic and balanced way of living, offering a roadmap for a more fulfilling and tranquil life.